WEIRD AND WONDERFUL
GROSS ANIMALS

TEXT BY
CRISTINA BANFI

ILLUSTRATIONS BY
ROSSELLA TRIONFETTI

WSkids
WHITE STAR KIDS

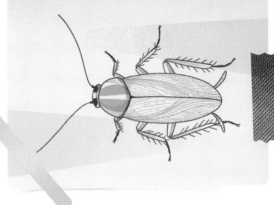

CONTENTS

INTRODUCTION

Incredible, but true!

Some animals appear to be completely **at ease** in the midst of vomit, spit, mud, and excrement.

You may mistakenly think this only applies to species that are generally considered disagreeable: spiders, snakes, toads... But there are also some **"unexpected"** ones: animals you thought were cute or graceful, never in a million years expecting them to be guilty of such nauseating behavior.

Would you ever have imagined, for example, that a giraffe uses its tongue to remove the **wax** from its ears? Or that there's a starfish that has to push its **stomach** out of its body to eat? And did you know that bees pass nectar to each other from mouth to mouth? Or that ants collect honeydew directly from an **aphid's anus**?!

Then there are animals that have a real taste for horror. Certain lizards can squirt **blood from their eyes** or detach **parts of their body**, and there are frogs that give birth through their **mouth** or **skin**! Other animals liquify their prey so they can suck them up like a **milkshake** or slowly devour their victims from the inside out, **like an evil alien.**

Herrings communicate by **farting**, and sometimes when hippos **poop**, they spin their tail to spray it everywhere! And there are some animals that do even more disgusting things, such as **eating their own poop**, like rabbits, or turning it into a pap to feed to their babies, as koalas do! But perhaps the grossest animals of all are those that **pee** out of their **mouth** or spray their urine far and wide.

YEAH!

You'll find a lot of distracting information in this entertaining book, but if you read it carefully—between those inevitable grimaces of disgust or chuckles of disbelief—you'll also discover the "**hidden**" truth.

That is, while at first many of these animal behaviors will just seem gross, you'll learn that they're actually important and cunning adaptations that help protect these species and are fundamental to their survival.

LLAMA

SCIENTIFIC NAME: *Lama glama*

DIET: *herbivore (eats plants)*

LENGTH: *4 ft (1.2 m)*

WEIGHT: *309 lbs (140 kg)*

HABITAT: *mountains*

LIFESPAN: *16 years*

REPRODUCTION: *after the females give birth to their young, they take care of them for a whole year*

GROSS FACT: *it spits saliva and vomits on anyone who annoys it*

We all know that spitting is rude, but for llamas it's a way of communicating with each other.

Any llama wanting to prove its superiority in the group will **spit on all the others** it deems to be of a lower rank so that they learn to recognize its authority.

Often, they **blow out air and saliva** when they're annoyed. Females, for example, might spit on a male that's coming on too strongly, warning him to leave her alone.

And if a llama gets really angry or feels threatened, it resorts to a far more deadly weapon. It **regurgitates** a truly smelly green fluid from its **stomach** and spits it, launching it up to **13 feet** (4 m). It then eats some aromatic leaves to get rid of the really bad taste in its mouth.

SACRED SCARAB

SCIENTIFIC NAME:
Scarabaeus sacer
DIET: *coprophagist (eats excrement)*
LENGTH: *1 in (2.5 cm)*
WEIGHT: *a few ounces*
HABITAT: *deserts*
LIFESPAN: *unknown*
REPRODUCTION: *the female deposits her eggs in balls of dung; it takes about two years for the larva to emerge as a fully developed beetle*
GROSS FACT: *it eats dung, inside which the baby beetles grow*

The sacred scarab, or dung beetle, has very peculiar tastes: indeed, its favorite food is **dung**, that is, the excrement left on the ground by herbivorous mammals, from which it extracts a **nutrient-rich liquid**. It can eat more than its own weight in just one day, thereby playing an important role in cleaning up the environment.

Scarabs also use dung to make cozy **nests** in which to **lay eggs**. They roll it along the ground, creating balls that are larger than their own bodies. They propel them with their hind legs, moving backwards, with their heads pointed at the ground.

The mom and dad help each other to roll the balls up to the entrance of a previously dug tunnel. After laying one egg in each ball, they push them inside. The dung then ferments, providing an **ideal environment** for the larvae to mature and enough **food** for them to develop into adults.

SKUNK

The skunk is a cute and friendly looking animal, but it keeps a terrible **secret** hidden underneath its bushy tail: two odoriferous glands, each no bigger than a grape, that it uses when it's in trouble or feels **threatened** by a potential predator.

SCIENTIFIC NAME: *Mephitis mephitis*

DIET: *omnivore (eats plants and the flesh of animals)*

LENGTH: *2.6 ft (80 cm)*

WEIGHT: *up to 13 lbs (6 kg)*

HABITAT: *forests and grasslands*

LIFESPAN: *3 years in the wild*

REPRODUCTION: *the females give birth in spring, and there can be as many as 10 kits in a litter*

GROSS FACT: *it sprays a foul-smelling liquid from its anal glands*

These glands produce an **oily yellow liquid** that has one of the most nauseating and repulsive smells in the entire animal kingdom. To bring the glands into action, the skunk turns its back on its opponent, raises its tail, and **squirts the liquid in its face** from as far away as 10 feet (3 m).

This stink bomb doesn't cause any serious harm to the skunk's attackers, but it does **disorientate** them and cause them to suffer for a long time afterward; the **terrible smell** lasts for days and days, and there is no way to get rid of it. This horrendous experience will be enough to ensure that the next time the attacker sees one of these black and white striped animals, it will do everything in its power to avoid it.

BOMBARDIER BEETLE

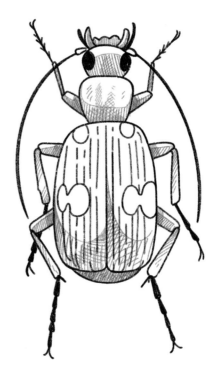

SCIENTIFIC NAME:
Pheropsophus jessoensis
DIET: *omnivore*
LENGTH: *1 in (2.5 cm)*
WEIGHT: *a few ounces*
HABITAT: *woods and grasslands*
LIFESPAN: *a few weeks*
REPRODUCTION: *the female lays its eggs among decaying leaves*
GROSS FACT: *it ejects hot toxic chemicals from the tip of its abdomen*

There are some animals that use **chemical weapons** to save their lives, and one of the most famous is the bombardier beetle. It reacts to danger by **firing explosives** out of the tip of its abdomen. This beetle has incredible aim and never misses its target.

The spray is a concoction of extremely **irritating** chemicals. Once released, they rapidly expand and heat to temperatures close to 212°F (100°C), the same as boiling water, and they can easily **burn** a hand.

It expels the gases like a **machine gun**, firing up to 500 pulses per second. If eaten by a toad, the insect can use its secret burning-hot weapon from inside the belly, forcing the predator to **vomit** its indigestible prey back up, alive and well.

TEXAS HORNED LIZARD

SCIENTIFIC NAME:
Phrynosoma cornutum

DIET: *insectivore (eats insects)*

LENGTH: *4.5 in (11 cm)*

WEIGHT: *3 oz (90 g)*

HABITAT: *arid areas*

LIFESPAN: *7 years (in captivity)*

REPRODUCTION: *the females lay their eggs in a nest dug in the sand; the hatchlings are independent immediately after birth*

GROSS FACT: *it squirts blood from its eyes*

This small lizard has a very squat, flat body, covered with spiny scales. There are two horns at the back of its head, which are extensions of its skull bones. Although it looks pretty terrifying, its small size and gentle nature make it a very docile animal.

The Texas horned lizard has two ways to defend itself against predators, especially coyotes. First, it can suck a large amount of air into its lungs to **inflate its body up to twice its normal size**. This makes all its **spines** stick out, and the lizard no longer looks like such an appetizing snack.

And if this proves insufficient, it employs a defense mechanism that's like something out of a horror movie: it squirts a directed **stream of blood** from small sacs in its **eyes** to a distance of up to 5 feet (1.5 m), aiming for the eyes of the attacker, so as to temporarily blind it.

HAIRY FROG

SCIENTIFIC NAME: *Trichobatrachus robustus*

DIET: *insectivore (eats insects)*

LENGTH: *4.5 in (11 cm)*

WEIGHT: *5.5 oz (150 g)*

HABITAT: *humid equatorial regions*

LIFESPAN: *unknown*

REPRODUCTION: *the females, which are smaller than the males, lay their eggs in streams, where they are protected by the males*

GROSS FACT: *it breaks the bones in its toes to defend itself*

As we know, frogs have smooth, bare skin. But during the breeding season, **male hairy frogs** grow **long, hair-like strands of skin** on their sides and back legs that contain lots of blood vessels. These are used to help absorb more oxygen, allowing the frogs to stay in the water longer and therefore protect and care for the eggs.

Don't be misled by this helpless looking African frog because it's hiding **an unexpected weapon.** When it feels threatened, it actively breaks the bones in its toes to create **sharp claws**, which puncture their way out of the toe pads.

Thanks to this defense mechanism, which is like something out of a horror movie, the hairy frog has earned the nickname "**Wolverine frog**," after the superhero who ejects long claws from his knuckles.

OCHRE SEA STAR

SCIENTIFIC NAME:
Pisaster ochraceus
DIET: carnivore (eats the flesh of animals)
LENGTH: up to 9.8 in (25 cm)
WEIGHT: uncalculated
HABITAT: rocky shores
LIFESPAN: 20 years
REPRODUCTION: the young are born from eggs, which are released into the water and left unprotected by the parents
GROSS FACT: it pushes its stomach out to digest prey larger than itself

Like many starfish, the ochre sea star is **carnivorous**. It feeds on various invertebrates, including **mussels and clams**. It's able to open the shells thanks to the powerful suction cups on each of its tube feet.

VALVE

However, once the valves are opened, it's unable to open its mouth wide enough to swallow such large prey. So, in order to feed, the sea star must use a mechanism that's astonishing, to say the least: if food can't get to its stomach, its stomach **goes to the food**.

STOMACH

It does this by **pushing its digestive system out** through its mouth and over its prey. It then starts digesting the soft body tissues, eventually turning them into soup. The stomach, and the partially digested prey, are then **retracted back into the body,** where digestion continues.

HIPPOPOTAMUS

It's a seemingly peaceful animal—a gentle giant. But the truth is, the hippopotamus is very **aggressive and irritable**. It attacks violently and unexpectedly, causing serious damage to those unfortunate enough to be on the receiving end. And then it also does something disgusting with its **excrement**.

When hippos emerge from the water, they spin their tails as they poop. This is the start of a competition to see who can **spray their poop the farthest**. Zoologists call this "**muck-spreading**." It's their way of marking their territory, scattering the feces over the largest possible area.

SCIENTIFIC NAME:
Hippopotamus amphibius
DIET: *herbivore (eats plants)*
LENGTH: *16.5 ft (5m)*
WEIGHT: *5 tons (4,500 kg)*
HABITAT: *forests*
LIFESPAN: *50 years*
REPRODUCTION: *After a gestation period of 8 months, the female gives birth to one calf that can weigh up to 110 lbs (50 kg)*
GROSS FACT: *it scatters its feces with its tail*

SPLATTER ZONE

Younger hippos also do this to **demonstrate their respect** for their older and stronger companions: **by spraying feces on their faces**, they confirm their submission and accept their dominance.

EUROPEAN RABBIT

Rabbits mainly eat grass, and like all animals they eliminate waste materials from the digestive tract through their poop, which they leave on the ground. Every day, they produce **about 300 small, round balls**, which are dark and fairly dry.

Rabbits also produce another type of poop—in private and usually at night—called **caecotroph**. This special poop is much softer, has a strong smell, and is also **a bit sticky**. You won't see these droppings lying around because the rabbit **eats them immediately**.

SCIENTIFIC NAME: *Oryctolagus cuniculus*
DIET: *herbivore (eats plants)*
LENGTH: *19.5 in (50 cm)*
WEIGHT: *5.5 lbs (2.5 kg)*
HABITAT: *woods*
LIFESPAN: *9 years*
REPRODUCTION: *the kittens are born in a den, blind, hairless, and helpless*
GROSS FACT: *it eats its own poop*

PHYSIOLOGICAL FECES   CAECOTROPHS

IS THAT A WEIRD HABIT, OR WHAT?

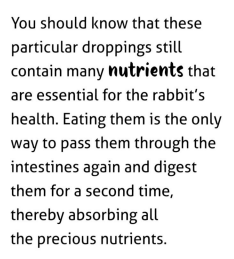

You should know that these particular droppings still contain many **nutrients** that are essential for the rabbit's health. Eating them is the only way to pass them through the intestines again and digest them for a second time, thereby absorbing all the precious nutrients.

LAMPREY

The river lamprey is a very strange creature that perhaps looks more like a snake than a fish. As an adult, **it's parasitic**, which means that it lives on another organism, in this case another fish, **slowly sucking out** its blood, tissues, and internal liquids until eventually it's reduced to an empty sack.

JAWLESS, ROUND MOUTH

SCIENTIFIC NAME:
Lampetra fluviatilis

DIET: carnivore (eats the flesh of animals)

LENGTH: 19.5 in (50 cm)

WEIGHT: 3.5 oz (100 g)

HABITAT: rivers

LIFESPAN: 10 years

REPRODUCTION: the female deposits up to 20,000 eggs, after which it dies.

GROSS FACT: they suck the blood and liquids from the body of their prey

The lamprey's round mouth has no jaws. It looks like a **suction cup** and is filled with lots of tiny sharp teeth. It uses its mouth to stay firmly attached—night and day—to the side or to the operculum over the gills of the host. The rows of sharp teeth, which also cover its tongue, are used to **grate a suction hole in the skin**.

There's no way for the fish to get rid of this uncomfortable guest, which over time will literally **suck the life out** of it. Once its job is done, the lamprey pulls away and swims off in search of another unfortunate host to suck to death.

LAMPREY

GIRAFFE

Giraffes don't just have long necks; **they also have long tongues.** The tongue can reach a length of **20 inches (50 cm)** and is also prehensile, which is very useful for collecting leaves.

SCIENTIFIC NAME:
Giraffa camelopardalis
DIET: *herbivore (eats plants)*
LENGTH: *18.5 ft (5.7 m)*
WEIGHT: *2.1 tons (1,900 kg)*
HABITAT: *savannas*
LIFESPAN: *25 years*
REPRODUCTION: *the mother gives birth standing up, so the newborn falls about 6 feet (2 m) to the ground*
GROSS FACT:
it cleans its ears and nose with its tongue

IT CAN BE AS LONG AS 20 INCHES!

A giraffe **can easily touch its ears** with its tongue, and—when necessary—clean them thoroughly by removing the earwax clogging the ear canal. And if this information isn't disgusting enough, imagine the giraffe then using the same tongue it cleaned its ears with to **pick its nose!**

It licks away all the snot, leaving the nostrils clear and clean. The saliva helps the tongue do a thorough cleaning job.

A giraffe's saliva is very thick, and it **contains antiseptic substances** that eliminate viruses and bacteria. It also completely disinfects small cuts, helping them to heal quickly.

SOUTHERN GASTRIC BROODING FROG

SCIENTIFIC NAME:
Rheobatrachus silus
DIET: *insectivore (eats insects)*
LENGTH: *2 in (5 cm)*
WEIGHT: *uncalculated*
HABITAT: *rain forests*
LIFESPAN: *3 years*
REPRODUCTION: *the female lays its eggs in gelatinous masses*

GROSS FACT:
the tadpoles develop in their mother's stomach, and she gives birth to them by vomiting

The southern gastric brooding frog is a small amphibian, resident of the rocky streams and natural pools in Australia's rain forests. Sadly, it has not been observed in nature for at least 30 years and is currently considered an extinct species.

The way it reproduced was quite astonishing, to say the least. The mother **swallowed her eggs**, about twenty of them; not to eat them, but **to protect them**. The eggs went directly **into her stomach**, which stopped producing hydrochloric acid to avoid digesting the tadpoles.

AUSTRALIAN RAIN FORESTS

THE BABY FROGS EMERGE

While the tadpoles were developing, which took 6 weeks, the mother stopped eating, and her belly grew bigger and bigger. When it was time to give birth, the female **vomited her baby frogs**.

TARANTULA HAWK

We all know that it's usually spiders that prey on insects, not the other way around. But the tarantula hawk is an exception. This insect is a **spider killer** because a mother's love knows no bounds! The female has just one goal: to search for the burrow of a big spider and to make sure that the occupant is at home. Once her goal is achieved, she plays tricks and moves the web at the entrance to convince the spider to come out.

SCIENTIFIC NAME:
Pepsis formosa
DIET: _the larvae are carnivorous; the adults eat pollen and nectar_
LENGTH: _1.8 in (4.5 cm)_
WEIGHT: _uncalculated_
HABITAT: _deserts_
LIFESPAN: _2 months_
REPRODUCTION: _it deposits eggs from which small carnivorous larvae hatch_
GROSS FACT: _the larva grows inside a big spider, which it eats alive_

As soon as the spider emerges, the female **stings it**, paralyzing it with her venom. Once the spider is no longer able to move, the wasp **drags** it into a hole and **buries** it alive by sealing the entrance, but not before **laying an egg** inside the body of her unlucky victim.

When the egg hatches, the spider is **still alive** but unable to move, and the tiny larva slowly **devours it from the inside out**.

THE LARVA DOESN'T EAT THE MAIN ORGANS RIGHT AWAY, SO AS TO KEEP ITS MEAL ALIVE FOR AS LONG AS POSSIBLE. THIS MEANS IT WILL HAVE ENOUGH FRESH FOOD TO LAST UNTIL IT METAMORPHOSES INTO AN ADULT WASP.

FULMAR

Chicks are generally small and helpless, but that's not the case with fulmars.

When attacked by a predator, which is perhaps convinced it's found an easy meal, they use an **astoundingly gross defense mechanism**, which is also **potentially dangerous** for the unsuspecting attacker.

Their secret weapon is **vomit bullets**, which they can shoot up to 5 feet (1.5 m), **directly into the face of** mice, foxes, seabirds, and anyone else who threatens them. They store an **oily, yellow liquid** in their stomach, which is so **foul-smelling** it makes their attackers feel really sick.

SCIENTIFIC NAME:
Fulmarus glacialis
DIET: *piscivore (eats fish)*
LENGTH: *19.5 in (50 cm)*
WEIGHT: *28 oz (800 g)*
HABITAT: *coastal areas*
LIFESPAN: *50 years*
REPRODUCTION: *the female lays one white egg in a fairly simple nest*
GROSS FACT: *the chicks vomit a stinky oil at predators*

When this oil is vomited onto a **feathered predator**, its **feathers stick together**. If the bird tries to wash it off in the ocean, it realizes —too late—that it's impossible to get rid of, and it ends up drowning.

THE VOMIT CAN REACH UP TO FIVE FEET.

ROCK PIGEON

SCIENTIFIC NAME: *Columba livia*
DIET: *omnivore (eats plants and the flesh of animals)*
LENGTH: *14 in (35 cm)*
WEIGHT: *12.5 oz (350 g)*
HABITAT: *parks and cities*
LIFESPAN: *6 years*
REPRODUCTION: *the female builds the nest and lays its eggs, usually 2, which are white*
GROSS FACT: *they regurgitate milk to feed their chicks*

You might think only mammals **produce milk**, but that's not true. Pigeons do, too, but because they don't have mammary glands, they do it in a slightly different way. Pigeon milk is produced **in the crop**, the sac attached to the esophagus, where food is stored before being digested.

When the chicks hatch, the crops of both parents change, and the skin that lines them **begins to flake**, a bit like dandruff.

But the detached cells aren't dry like dandruff. They contain a **nutritious liquid** that's rich in proteins and fats.

CROP

To feed the chicks, the milk must be **regurgitated**, and for over two weeks it is the **only nourishment** the hatchlings receive. Flamingos and male emperor penguins also produce crop milk.

SURINAME TOAD

SCIENTIFIC NAME: *Pipa pipa*
DIET: carnivore (eats the flesh of animals)
LENGTH: 7 in (18 cm)
WEIGHT: 5.3 oz (150 g)
HABITAT: wet areas
LIFESPAN: 6–8 years
REPRODUCTION: the females lay 60–100 eggs
GROSS FACT: the young develop in the skin of the female's back

Just looking at this toad is enough to gross you out. Its brown body is **so flat it looks more like a rotting leaf** than an amphibian. The skin is covered with **wart-like bumps** and is **slimy and slippery.**

The way it reproduces is even more disgusting.

UNLIKE MOST AMPHIBIANS, THEY DON'T LAY THEIR EGGS IN A POOL OF WATER. THEY ARE STUCK TO THE MOTHER'S BACK, AND THEY SLOWLY SINK INTO THE SKIN, WHICH GROWS UP AND AROUND THEM TO CREATE POCKETS.

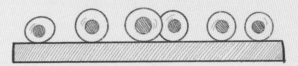

DEPOSITED EGGS

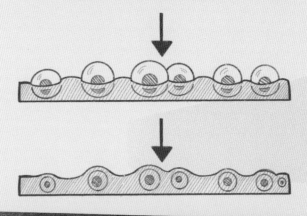

Three or four months later, when the mother sheds her skin, the young toads **burst out of her back**. They are fully formed and look like the adults, although they are only about half an inch (1 cm) long.

TURKEY VULTURE

SCIENTIFIC NAME: *Cathartes aura*

DIET: *carnivore (eats the flesh of animals)*

LENGTH: *2.5 ft (80 cm)*

WEIGHT: *4.5 lbs (2 kg)*

HABITAT: *savannas and forests*

LIFESPAN: *15–20 years*

REPRODUCTION: *the chicks are fed by both parents, and if they are in danger, they pretend to be dead*

GROSS FACT: *it poops and pees on itself*

There are some animals that have a good reason for **pooping or peeing on themselves**. The turkey vulture, like many other species of vultures, **poops and pees on its legs**, and the more there is, the better.

The acids in its excrement act like a **disinfectant**, killing all the bacteria that collect on the bird's feet as it steps on and scavenges **putrid carcasses**. Its **urine**, on the other hand, **cools down** its dirty legs as it evaporates, providing a little relief on scorching hot days.

Sometimes, the inevitable stench is even stronger. On top of the stinky poop, there's also the **acidic smell** of partially digested food, which the vulture **vomits** on those who disturb it. Due to the gastric juices it contains, it really burns.

VAMPIRE BAT

Contrary to what the legend of Count Dracula says, ordinary bats do not suck the blood of humans. That said, in South America there's one bat that only feeds on the blood of other animals, especially birds and livestock, such as horses and cows.

It surprises them at night, while they sleep, making a **small, painless incision** with its sharp teeth, usually on the leg. It then gently licks the blood that flows from the wound. Its saliva contains a protein called **draculin**, which ensures that the blood of its prey remains liquid, preventing a scab from forming too quickly on the open wound.

SCIENTIFIC NAME: *Desmodus rotundus*
DIET: *blood*
LENGTH: *2.5–3.5 in (6–9 cm)*
WEIGHT: *1.2 oz (33 g)*
HABITAT: *varies from dry to wet*
LIFESPAN: *12 years*
REPRODUCTION: *the females give birth in a cave, usually to just one pup*
GROSS FACT: *it feeds on blood*

IT CONTAINS A PROTEIN CALLED DRACULIN

It has a **heat-sensing organ** inside its nose that helps the bat find the blood vessels under the skin of its victim. It draws just one tablespoon of blood for each meal. If a vampire bat doesn't eat for two nights in a row, it dies of starvation.

RED DEER

A male deer's large, multi-pointed horns are called **antlers**. They're made of bone and are shed once a year, at the end of winter. The antlers start to grow back in spring, and by the end of summer they are fully grown. They can reach a length of 3.3 feet (1 m), and weigh up to 22 pounds (10 kg).

ANTLERS WITHOUT VELVET

THE ANTLERS ARE SHED

ANTLERS IN VELVET

THE ANTLERS ARE STRIPPED CLEAN

SCIENTIFIC NAME: *Cervus elaphus*
DIET: *herbivore (eats plants)*
LENGTH: *6.6 ft (2 m)*
WEIGHT: *550 lbs (250 kg)*
HABITAT: *temperate woods and forests*
LIFESPAN: *18 years*
REPRODUCTION: *1 or 2 fawns are born, with brown fur and white spots that will disappear when they are three months old*
GROSS FACT: *it peels the velvet off its antlers*

The red deer uses its antlers to attract females, as well as to protect itself against other males during the mating season. Sometimes, the males fight each other to show their strength by locking their antlers in a **head-to-head duel**.

While growing, the antlers are covered in velvet, a very sensitive, **fuzzy-looking skin** that is packed with **blood vessels**. It nourishes the bone tissue until the antlers are fully developed. Once the velvet has completed its task, it dies and dries up. It gradually sheds, leaving the deer with **bloody strips** of tissue **dangling off** its antlers.

BLACK WIDOW SPIDER

Like all spiders, the black widow is a **ferocious hunter**, and many different animals can end up in her clutches, even small snakes. It captures its prey by **trapping them in its web**, the strands of which are extremely strong and long enough to touch the ground.

SCIENTIFIC NAME: *Latrodectus mactans*
DIET: *insectivore (eats insects)*
LENGTH: *9 in (23 cm)*
WEIGHT: *0.035 oz (1 g)*
HABITAT: *damp environments*
LIFESPAN: *5 years*
REPRODUCTION: *the female lays 2–4 eggs, which hatch after about two weeks*
GROSS FACT: *it sucks up the body of its prey, after dissolving its tissues with venom*

HELP!

Once the victim has fallen into the trap, the spider bites it, injecting it with its **deadly venom**, which immediately **paralyzes** the prey. The black widow then calmly wraps it up in its silk and **drags it up** to its nest.

AT MEALTIMES, THE SPIDER SUCKS IT UP LIKE A MILKSHAKE. THE DIGESTIVE ENZYMES IN THE VENOM LIQUIFY THE SOFT PARTS OF THE PREY, WHICH ALLOWS THE SPIDER TO FEED ON IT FOR DAYS, AND SOMETIMES EVEN WEEKS.

SCIENTIFIC NAME: *Bison bonasus*

DIET: *herbivore (eats plants)*

LENGTH: *9.5 ft (2.9 m)*

WEIGHT: *1,764 lbs (800 kg)*

HABITAT: *forests*

LIFESPAN: *24 years*

REPRODUCTION: *usually just one calf is born, and half an hour later it stands up and follows its mother*

GROSS FACT: *it regurgitates the grass it's eaten into its mouth and produces large quantities of intestinal gases*

Bison, like antelopes, giraffes, camels, deer, and many other herbivorous mammals, are ruminants, that is, they have a **special stomach** that is divided into four compartments. The largest is called the **rumen**, and it acts as storage for vegetation that is eaten quickly and only coarsely chewed.

The animal can then **regurgitate the food** into its mouth and chew it in peace and quiet for as long as 6–8 hours. It produces about **26 gallons (100 liters) of saliva** to help it swallow and completely digest the food. The entire process can take up to **4 days**.

There are also numerous **bacteria** in the stomach that aid digestion. However, as these microorganisms do their job, they produce large quantities of **intestinal gases**, including methane and carbon dioxide. Alas, in addition to being pestilential, the farts produced by ruminants contribute to the greenhouse effect.

WILD BOAR

SCIENTIFIC NAME: *Sus scrofa*

DIET: *omnivore (eats plants and the flesh of animals)*

LENGTH: *8 ft (2.4 m)*

WEIGHT: *440 lbs (200 kg)*

HABITAT: *forests*

LIFESPAN: *13 years*

REPRODUCTION: *only the mother takes care of the piglets, on average 7–8 per litter*

GROSS FACT: *it rolls around in the mud*

What could be dirtier than **rolling around in the mud**, getting completely covered from head to toe? Baby wild boars love doing it, without the risk of being told to stop; on the contrary, **they are encouraged** by their moms, who show them exactly how it's done.

That's not to say that wild boars actually like dirt: they simply don't want **fleas, ticks, or fly eggs nesting in their fur**. And because they don't like being bitten by horseflies either, they know that a nice layer of mud will keep these pesky insects away from their skin.

On very hot days, a nice bath in dirty water **is really cooling**, and the feeling lasts longer because muddy water evaporates more slowly than clean water. Of course, we can't rule out the possibility that wild boars sometimes just roll around in the mud because they enjoy it!

BENEFITS

RED OVENBIRD

Home sweet home! The red ovenbird uses whatever material it can find to **build its nest**. It prefers **clay**, but if it can't find any, it's quite happy to use **manure** collected from the fields.

SCIENTIFIC NAME: *Furnarius rufus*

DIET: *insectivore (eats insects)*

LENGTH: *8 in (20 cm)*

WEIGHT: *2 oz (55 g)*

HABITAT: *grasslands*

LIFESPAN: *16 years*

REPRODUCTION: *the female lays between 2 to 4 eggs in the nest, which are then brooded by both parents*

GROSS FACT: *it builds its nest with manure*

Like a skilled little builder, this little bird first **makes a paste of poop, mud, and straw.** Then, on the branch of a tree or on top of a pole, it makes a domed nest, about 8 inches (20 cm) wide, which looks like an old-fashioned wood-fired oven, hence its curious name.

Once the job is finished, the bird lets the sun slowly dry its new home, so as to make it solid. Over time, **the stench of the poop fades,** and the chicks are reared in the inner chamber, on a bed of dry grass, tufts of fur, and wads of cotton.

SPITTLEBUG

SCIENTIFIC NAME:
Philaenus spumarius
DIET: *herbivore (eats plants)*
LENGTH: *0.2–0.3 in (5–7 mm)*
WEIGHT: *uncalculated*
HABITAT: *grasslands and woods*
LIFESPAN: *a few months*
REPRODUCTION: *the female lays its eggs in fall, under the bark of trees, so as to protect them during winter*
GROSS FACT: *it lives in a substance similar to spit*

Its name is enough to understand what's gross about this insect. The nymphs are born in spring and immediately colonize the tender seedlings sprouting out of the ground. They guzzle up the sap, sucking it out of the plant with their rostrum.

WHAT'S GROSS ABOUT THAT?

The small and defenseless nymphs build a shelter to **protect themselves from predators**. Not only does it keep them hidden, but it also creates an **ideal temperature**, both in bad weather and on very hot days, when they risk drying out.

This hiding place is made of a **foamy substance** that they make themselves. They have a special valve on their abdomen, which pumps air bubbles into the **liquid waste produced by the intestine.** The result is a soft, foamy mass that looks just like spit.

HOUSEFLY

SCIENTIFIC NAME:
Musca domestica
DIET: *omnivore (eats plants and the flesh of animals)*
LENGTH: *0.3 in (0.7 cm)*
WEIGHT: *0.0004 oz (0.012 g)*
HABITAT: *urban and rural areas*
LIFESPAN: *28 days*
REPRODUCTION: *it deposits hundreds of eggs, which hatch into larvae called maggots*
GROSS FACT: *it vomits on food and also eats poop*

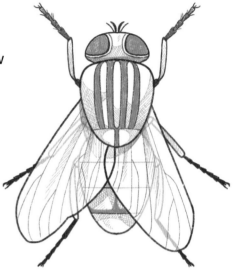

A fly can eat anything, but it can't chew with the small proboscis on its mouth. When it lands on a slice of cake, or on top of dung, **it spits regurgitated digestives juices onto its meal** and waits for it to dissolve before sucking it up.

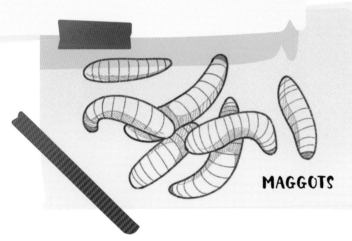

MAGGOTS

To make sure the food is good, **it tastes it with its feet**; when a fly finds something that could be edible, it tramples on it for a long time, **walking back and forth**. So, remember this: If you see a fly walking on your cookies, it may have just come from a pile of poop!

Flies have a very fast digestive system and therefore have to **poop frequently**. They probably do so every time they land, even on their own food.

IF YOU ARE NOT GROSSED OUT ENOUGH YET, KNOWING THAT FLIES ARE BORN IN MANURE OR INSIDE A DEAD BODY SHOULD DO THE TRICK!

SAND TIGER SHARK

It's normal for siblings to quarrel, but for these sharks that's not enough. They're capable of **eating each other** before they are even born, when they are still **in their mother's womb**, without her even noticing.

SCIENTIFIC NAME: *Carcharias taurus*

DIET: *carnivore (eats the flesh of animals)*

LENGTH: *10.5 ft (3.2 m)*

WEIGHT: *220 lbs (100 kg)*

HABITAT: *tropical and temperate oceans*

LIFESPAN: *35 years*

REPRODUCTION: *the females give birth to two baby sharks, each about 3.3 feet (1 m) long*

GROSS FACT:
they eat their brothers and sisters while still in the womb

While 12 littermates may start out in their mother's womb, as soon as the embryos grow their very sharp teeth, **the two largest pups eat their smaller siblings** one by one, before the mother even gives birth.

It's not an evil act; this form of cannibalism within a litter is a way to guarantee that **at least two of the developing pups** have enough energy to be born strong and healthy, and therefore relatively safe from other predators.

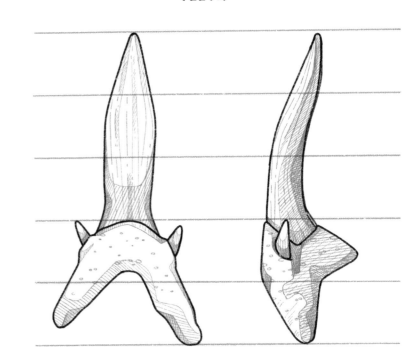

ORIENTAL COCKROACH

Cockroaches, by nature, are **gross**. They frequent dirty environments and are unwanted guests in the kitchen, where they seek food to satisfy their insatiable hunger. They spend time in **trash cans and garbage**, and therefore easily spread germs and bacteria.

SCIENTIFIC NAME: *Blatta orientalis*

DIET: *omnivore (eats plants and the flesh of animals)*

LENGTH: *1.3 in (3.3 cm)*

WEIGHT: *0.03 oz (0.95 g)*

HABITAT: *any*

LIFESPAN: *12–18 months*

REPRODUCTION: *the females produce a capsule that is about half an inch (1 cm) long, which contains about 15 eggs*

GROSS FACT: *it can live without its head for 7 days*

Even more terrifying, an oriental cockroach can stay alive even after **losing its head!** Being an insect, it doesn't breathe through the mouth, but through little holes in its body. Furthermore, it doesn't bleed to death because its blood— or more accurately, its hemolymph—is at low pressure, and therefore it doesn't bleed out from the wound too quickly, leaving enough time for a scab to form where its head used to be.

The body's nervous tissues will continue to function **even if the brain is lost** with the head, allowing the insect to live a fairly normal life. It dies of dehydration about **seven days later** because the oriental cockroach cannot survive longer than that without water.

THERE ARE 4,000 SPECIES OF COCKROACHES, OF DIFFERENT SIZES AND WITH DIFFERENT HABITATS:

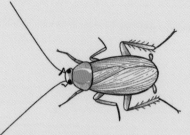

BROWN-BANDED COCKROACH

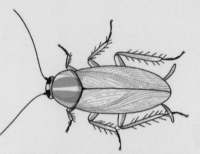

GERMAN COCKROACH

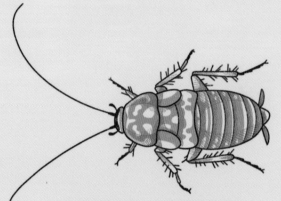

HARLEQUIN COCKROACH

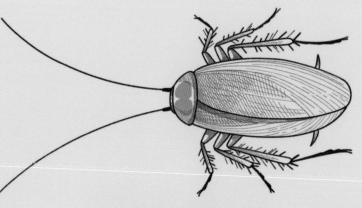

AMERICAN COCKROACH

ANT

Ants are social little creatures. They live in a colony, carrying out different jobs for the well-being of the entire community. One of their jobs is to **farm aphids**, small insects that feed on plant sap.

SCIENTIFIC NAME: *Hymenoptera*

DIET: *omnivore (eats plants and the flesh of animals)*

LENGTH: *0.04–0.98 in (1–25 mm)*

WEIGHT: *average 0.00014 oz (4 mg)*

HABITAT: *any, except glaciers*

LIFESPAN: *2–3 years; queen can live up to 30 years*

REPRODUCTION: *the queen is the only ant in the colony to lay eggs*

GROSS FACT: *they eat honeydew from the anuses of aphids*

The ants take very good care of them. They protect them from predators and the cold, take them to the best plants, and "**pamper**" them by stroking them with their antennas. In exchange, the ants get **droplets of honeydew**, a sticky substance rich in sugars, which they can't get enough of.

Aphids excrete honeydew as waste. In other words, it's **their poop.** And the ants don't waste any time: They **lick it up greedily** the moment it leaves the aphid's body, literally in ecstasy.

APHID

BEE

When two bees meet inside the beehive and approach each other, it often looks like **they're kissing**. It may seem like a show of affection between sisters, but they're actually feeding each other, **passing the food** from mouth to mouth.

This process is called **trophallaxis**, and it is also used by the worker bees that take care of **the queen**. After licking her for quite a while, they pass on some of **her essence** to their companions, thereby letting the entire colony know that the queen is alive and in excellent health.

SCIENTIFIC NAME:
Apis mellifera
DIET: *pollen, nectar, and honey*
LENGTH: *0.8 in (2 cm)*
WEIGHT: *0.007 oz/0.19 g (queen)*
HABITAT: *agricultural areas*
LIFESPAN: *worker 30 days; queen 5 years*
REPRODUCTION: *in a colony, only the queen bee deposits eggs, and the larvae are then fed and cared for by the worker bees*
GROSS FACT: *food is passed mouth to mouth from bee to bee*

Unfortunately, trophallaxis can also aid in the **spread of diseases** caused by microorganisms that reside inside the intestines. They are passed through the mouth and can infect other individuals in the colony, making them very sick.

LIGULA

COMMON WALL LIZARD

SCIENTIFIC NAME: *Podarcis muralis*

DIET: *carnivore (eats the flesh of animals)*

LENGTH: *8 in (20 cm)*

WEIGHT: *0.2 oz (6 g)*

HABITAT: *rocky and urban areas*

LIFESPAN: *10 years*

REPRODUCTION: *the female lays between 2 and 10 eggs in soil or under flat stones, so that the heat of the sun can reach them*

GROSS FACT: *it can self-amputate its tail, which continues to move even after it has detached from the body*

THE LIZARD FREQUENTLY LOSES A PIECE OF ITS BODY, IN A GRUESOME WAY! The lizard **drops its tail** when it fears it's being attacked. The tail continues to move back and forth, distracting the attacker while the reptile quickly runs away.

Although it may sound like something from a horror movie, it's actually a defense mechanism that can save the lizard's life. When bites or scratches aren't enough, the lizard self-amputates its tail, which it leaves **for the predator to eat**.

BETTER TO NOT HAVE A TAIL, THAN NOT HAVE A LIFE!

Losing its tail isn't painful for the reptile because the muscles naturally pull away from one another along the fracture plane, which is a weak point. The tail is replaced by a brand new one, which **grows back** little by little, although it's slighter **smaller and less flexible**.

WOMBAT

The wombat is a small, funny-looking marsupial that lives in **Australian forests**, inside long tunnels it digs in the ground.

It **looks adorable**, with its little chubby body and squat legs, but it has a gross little a secret: it's the only animal in the world to **poop cubes**.

Scientists have discovered that wombats take **2 and a half weeks** to digest the plants they eat and that their poop only solidifies in the last 8 centimeters of the intestine. This is where it turns into **cubes**, each side of which measures about **0.7 inches (2 cm)**.

SCIENTIFIC NAME:
Vombatus ursinus
DIET: *herbivore (eats plants)*
LENGTH: *3.3 ft (1 m)*
WEIGHT: *77 lbs (35 kg)*
HABITAT: *forests*
LIFESPAN: *15 years*
REPRODUCTION: *the female gives birth every two years and then carries the joey in its pouch for 6 months*
GROSS FACT: *it poops cubes*

It can produce more than **100 cubes of poop** in one night. The wombat then uses them like bricks, placing them **around the entrance of its den**. It does this to make the opening smaller, but also to show other animals that the house is already occupied.

LION

The lion is a truly majestic animal, a symbol of strength, courage, and wisdom. However, it has one bad habit that's extremely distasteful: it goes around **spraying jets of pee** on tree trunks, boulders, and bushes, from as far as **10 feet (3 m)** away.

Like many felines, this is one of the ways a lion marks its territory. The other is by roaring loudly. It uses its urine to leave **foul-smelling messages** on specific points along its territory's borders.

SCIENTIFIC NAME:
Panthera leo
DIET: *carnivore (eats the flesh of animals)*
LENGTH: *8 ft (2.5 m)*
WEIGHT: *420 lbs (190 kg)*
HABITAT: *savannas*
LIFESPAN: *18 years*
REPRODUCTION: *several females belonging to the same pride can give birth in the same period, and the cubs are often raised in creches*
GROSS FACT: *it sprays urine to mark its territory*

So, a lion's pee has two functions: It **eliminates waste** from the body, and it helps it to communicate with other lions. **Both sexes** start spraying pee when they're about 2 years old, although males do it far more often than females.

BABOON

When a female baboon wants to be noticed, she shows off **her butt,** which swells into **a fleshy mass** that's as red as a bell pepper, making it even more visible.

IT'S IMPOSSIBLE FOR A BUTT LIKE THIS TO GO UNNOTICED!

Males looking to start a family, **go crazy** when they see a female's huge red butt, and they even **become aggressive** toward any rivals.

At the end of the mating period, the female's swelling goes down, and life returns to normal. That is, until the next time a male baboon catches her eye.

WE DON'T KNOW HOW COMFORTABLE IT IS TO CARRY SUCH A BIG BUTT AROUND, BUT IT SURE LOOKS LIKE A GREAT CUSHION TO SIT ON.

53

CHINESE SOFTSHELL TURTLE

SCIENTIFIC NAME:
Pelodiscus sinensis
DIET: *carnivore (eats the flesh of animals)*
LENGTH: *13 in (33 cm)*
WEIGHT: *5.5 lbs (2.5 kg)*
HABITAT: *freshwater environments*
LIFESPAN: *50 years*
REPRODUCTION: *the females lay between 8 and 30 eggs, with a diameter of about 0.8 in (20 mm), up to 5 times a year*
GROSS FACT: *it pees out of its mouth*

Peeing out of the mouth may seem like an unhygienic habit to us, and even a little nauseating, but in the animal world, there's a reptile for which it's quite normal. It lives in **salty swamps,** and it's called the Chinese softshell turtle.

THE CARAPACE IS COVERED IN SOFT, LEATHERY SKIN.

It spends most of its time submerged in water, where it pees a small amount of urea in the normal way. It expels the rest of its liquid waste when it's on land, but instead of finding a small bush behind which to pee, this turtle **goes looking for a puddle**.

It **plunges its head into the water** and then **rhythmically expands and contracts its mouth** to excrete the urine. Once the turtle's finished, it rinses its mouth and continues on its way, as if it was a perfectly normal thing to do.

SCIENTIFIC NAME:
Phascolarctos cinereus
DIET: *herbivore (eats plants)*
LENGTH: *33.5 in (85 cm)*
WEIGHT: *33 lbs (15 kg)*
HABITAT: *eucalyptus forests*
LIFESPAN: *20 years*
REPRODUCTION: *the female usually gives birth to just one joey at a time, which climbs into its mother's pouch and stays there for up to 6 months*
GROSS FACT: *the newborn joey eats its mother's poop, which contains enzymes to aid its digestion of eucalyptus leaves*

EUCALYPTUS

KOALA

Eucalyptus leaves are hard, fibrous, and poisonous and therefore practically **impossible** for most animals **to digest**. But not for the koala. This cute marsupial has **special bacteria** in its intestine, which allow it to absorb the nutrients.

Joeys aren't born with these microorganisms, so before they can eat eucalyptus leaves, they must first receive this **intestinal flora** from their mother. So, how do they get it? In the grossest way you can possibly imagine: **BY EATING HER POOP.**

The joey sticks its head out of the pouch, and waits for its mother to produce some really **soft poop** that's full of gut bacteria. Having eaten this rather bizarre pap, the joey is ready to **start weaning**.

JULIA BUTTERFLY

Like all butterflies, the Julia butterfly sucks nectar out of flowers through its proboscis.
However, **mineral salts** are also important in any diet, and if they can't be found in the soil, it's necessary to look for them elsewhere.

The easiest source for this butterfly is found **in the eyes** of the fearsome caiman, a crocodilian; **its tears**, like ours, are salty because they contain **sodium**. The butterfly has learned how to sip them very gently, settled fearlessly on the huge reptile's head.

SCIENTIFIC NAME: *Dryas iulia*
DIET: *nectar*
APERTURA ALARE: *3.5 in (9 cm)*
WEIGHT: *0.007 oz (0.195 g)*
HABITAT: *forests*
LIFESPAN: *36 days*
REPRODUCTION: *the eggs are laid individually, and the caterpillars feed on leaves*
GROSS FACT: *it drinks the tears of the caiman*

CATERPILLAR

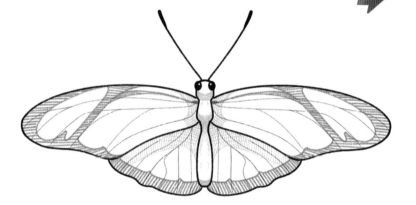

If the caiman's eyes are dry, the Julia butterfly deliberately **starts irritating them** to get the caiman to produce enough tears for it to sip up its ration of salt.

EGYPTIAN PLOVER

SCIENTIFIC NAME:
Pluvianus aegyptius

DIET: *carnivore*
(eats the flesh of animals)

LENGTH: *8 in (20 cm)*

WEIGHT: *3 oz (85 g)*

HABITAT: *lowland tropical rivers*

LIFESPAN: *6 years*

REPRODUCTION: *it deposits two to three eggs, which on very hot days both parents frequently soak with water to keep them cool*

GROSS FACT: *it goes into a crocodile's mouth and picks out the decaying meat stuck in its teeth*

HOW MUCH COURAGE DO YOU NEED TO GO INSIDE THE OPEN JAWS OF A CROCODILE?

The Egyptian plover has more than enough, but it also knows that the ferocious reptile will stay still and motionless, as if it were at the dentist having its teeth cleaned.

The tiny bird inspects the crocodile's open mouth thoroughly, checking to see if there are any pieces of **stinky flesh** caught between its teeth, perhaps already decaying and infecting the gums.

Of course, the plover gets **something in return**: an **easy meal** to supplement its diet. It may not be very fresh, but it can certainly be eaten in a **safe place**:

NO PREDATOR WOULD EVER DARE TO BOTHER IT WHILE IT'S INSIDE ITS PROTECTOR'S MOUTH.

HERRING

The herring is a very common silver fish. They live in an enormous shoal made up of thousands of individuals, in the temperate waters of the Pacific and Atlantic Oceans. During the day, the herrings stay in deep water, while at sunset, when there are less predators swimming around, they rise to the surface and swim with their mouths open, collecting **plankton**.

SCIENTIFIC NAME: *Clupea harengus*

DIET: *plankton*

LENGTH: *12 in (30 cm)*

WEIGHT: *35 oz (1 kg)*

HABITAT: *temperate oceans*

LIFESPAN: *3–4 years*

REPRODUCTION: *females can lay up to 40,000 eggs, which they deposit on rocks or aquatic plants*

GROSS FACT: *it communicates by blowing bubbles out of its butt*

PLANKTON

In order to stay together when night falls, **they release** a stream of bubbles and farting noises **from their anuses**. The bubbles and noises are their way of staying in contact, making it easy for them to find each other, even in the dark.

Since other fish are unable to understand these curious signals, herrings can safely **communicate with each other**, without the risk of attracting predators.

SNAIL

SCIENTIFIC NAME:
Helix pomatia
DIET: *herbivore (eats plants)*
LENGTH: *2 in (5 cm)*
WEIGHT: *0.35 oz (10 g)*
HABITAT: *grasslands and woods*
LIFESPAN: *10 years*
REPRODUCTION: *they bury up to 30 eggs, covering them with mucus and soil*
GROSS FACT: *it moves by sliding on its own saliva*

THE BENEFITS OF SALIVA

Mucus is a thick, sticky fluid. Even the thought of touching it is gross, and yet there are animals that are quite happy to **cover their bodies** in it. The snail, for example, produces large quantities, which it leaves in a silvery trail behind it.

This slimy substance reduces evaporation, thereby keeping the snail's body **moist**, soft, and supple, preventing it from drying out. It's also a **defense** against harmful bacteria, sunlight, and wounds that the snail might get as it moves over stony ground.

As you can imagine, the mucus is also very slippery, so the snail uses it as **a trail to glide over**. When it stops to rest, the mucus **becomes sticky** so that the snail can stay stuck on any type of surface, even if it's vertical.

MILLIPEDE

SCIENTIFIC NAME:
Pachyiulus communis
DIET: *detritivore (eats dead organisms and wastes)*
LENGTH: *2.5 in (6 cm)*
WEIGHT: *0.1 oz (2.5 g)*
HABITAT: *wet areas*
LIFESPAN: *7 years*
REPRODUCTION: *the females lay their eggs in holes dug in the soil*
GROSS FACT: *it releases an irritating and foul-smelling secretion*

The millipede's wormlike body, is actually made up of lots of articulated segments. Attached to these, there are 300 legs—not 1,000 as its name suggests—that are so short that it's impossible for it to run very fast. Besides not being even remotely beautiful, this animal also has some pretty bad habits: it likes living in **damp places** and eating **decaying vegetables**.

The way it looks is actually its least gross characteristic; it releases a **yellowish, acrid, and toxic fluid** from the sides of its body, which contains a **powerful venom** called hydrocyanic acid. It can irritate the skin and damage the eyes, as well as leave a disgusting smell.

This nauseating fluid is a way to ward off anyone who disturbs it. When attacked, the millipede **curls up into a ball**, hoping it will be left in peace. And if that doesn't work, it uses its **secret weapon**, knowing that disgusting, foul-smelling meals are far from popular.

ROSSELLA TRIONFETTI

As a child, Rossella would go to book shops and libraries in search of illustrated books on animals, immediately showing her interest in drawing the world around her. After graduating in Applied Arts, she specialized in the field of illustration and graphics by attending various courses with professionals in the sector, including the MiMaster of Milan. She currently works as an illustrator of children's books, also collaborating in the creation of apps and interactive games. In recent years, she has illustrated several books for White Star Kids.

CRISTINA BANFI

Cristina has a degree in Natural Sciences from the University of Milan and has taught in several schools. She has been involved in scientific communication and fun learning for over 20 years and has contributed to numerous school textbooks and educational publications, mainly for children and adolescents. In recent years, she has written several books for White Star.

White Star Kids™ is a trademark of White Star s.r.l.

© 2022 White Star s.r.l.
Piazzale Luigi Cadorna, 6
20123 Milan, Italy
www.whitestar.it

Translation: TperTradurre, Rome, Italy
Editing: Michele Suchomel-Casey

Second printing, March 2023

ISBN 978-88-544-1912-4
2 3 4 5 6   27 26 25 24 23

Printed and manufactured in China by
Dream Colour (Hong Kong) Printing Limited.

FSC
www.fsc.org
MIX
Paper from
responsible sources
FSC® C178000